After West

ALSO BY JAMES HARMS

Freeways and Aqueducts
Quarters
The Joy Addict
Modern Ocean

Limited Editions
East of Avalon
L.A. Afterglow

After West

poems by
James Harms

Carnegie Mellon University Press
Pittsburgh 2008

Acknowledgments

My thanks to the editors of the following journals and anthologies where some of these poems first appeared, occasionally in earlier versions:

ABZ ("Our Fathers," "She Said"), *Alligator Juniper* ("An Accordion in Autumn"), *Bat City Review* ("Knowing You Were Loved"), *Blue Moon Review* ("February"), *Caffeine Destiny* ("Your Favorite Things"), *Canary* ("Nothing New but Everything"), *Cimarron Review* ("If Afternoon"), *Crazyhorse* ("Spring in Lincoln Park, 1910"), *The Gettysburg Review* ("On Beauty and West Virginia at the Blue Moose Café"), *Hotel Amerika* ("Held Down"), *Hunger Mountain* ("Elegy by Frank Gehry," "If I Could Break Down Anywhere it Would Be Halfway to Todos Santos," "Love Poem by Frank Gehry"), *Indiana Review* ("Tribe and Country"), *Kestrel* ("Days"), *Nightsun* ("As If"), *The North American Review* ("After West (Pastoral by Frank Gehry)"), *Ploughshares* ("Like Mercury, the Monongahela"), *Poetry International* ("Isn't That Enough"), *Red, White and Blues: Poets on the Promise of America* ("After West (1-8, 10-12, 14-15)"), *Rivendell* ("Breakfast in West Virginia," "When Dean Left West Virginia," "Mountaintop Removal, Wallace Stevens, My Son Walt, West Virginia"), *Shenandoah* ("Pisgah Church Cemetery"), *Smartish Pace* ("The Difficult Science of Separation," "Phoebe at Daybreak"), *Sycamore Review* ("Comedy: Morgantown, West Virginia," "For Ashes, For Letting Go"), *Tar River Poetry* ("A Friday at the End of August," "Landscape as the Latest Diet"), *Verse* ("My Dream of Bob Marley" — also appeared in *Jacket*)

"Landscape as the Latest Diet" also appeared in *Poets on Place*, edited by W.T. Pfefferle. "Pisgah Church Cemetery" also appeared in *Under the Rock Umbrella: Contemporary American Poets from 1951 to 1977*, edited by William Walsh. "Breakfast in West Virginia" also appeared in *Coal: A Poetry Anthology*, edited by Chris Green and Edwina Pendarvis.

Contents

IN MEMORY OF AGNES, PEGGY & HEARN

Long having wander'd since, round the earth having wander'd,
Now I face home again, very pleas'd and joyous,
(But where is what I started for so long ago?
And why is it yet unfound?)

–Walt Whitman

ONE

Pisgah Church Cemetery

Morgantown, West Virginia

They came down to the shore
in wood-paneled Fords, the land yachts
of old, the twin-finned and two-toned,
flared wheel wells, chrome grillwork,
the loveliest fenders since all Detroit
turned back from making planes
to the central task, the business
of business. And then the children
were born. The lawns, the plastic
pink flamingos, small towns
and suburbs, the movement west,
the drift of labor, a job here, a rumor
there, coal and steel along the river,
more children, grandchildren.
It will take centuries, won't it,
to fill our graveyards, but then?—
a revision of our fondness
for the lost, a recognition:
we can stack the dead, fill further
the cramped yard behind the chapel
south of town, the murmuring river
beyond the woods, where your ancestors
the Frums breathe mist into October mornings.
To be found forever, even when the wind
has softened our names, the stone
a vague cloud propped upright in the grass,
even when there is no one left
to find us. Forever. They came down
to the river at dusk to wait
for the fireworks, the concert under stars.
It was a century of loss, though not
for us, we who gathered innumerably
near water to work or wonder, to wait.

We who wait to be visited are certain
of memory. Certain we existed.
It was a century of loss, yes, and all of it
was ours. Remember me. I promise
I'll remember you. And after that?
Let's let tomorrow take care of tomorrow.
Let tomorrow lie down on today.

On Beauty and West Virginia at the Blue Moose Café

The Monongahela flows north at the will
of Mellons and Carnegies to join
the Allegheny and the Ohio, to give away
its name and what's left of
West Virginia coal and limestone to
our beloved Pittsburgh, vanishing point
of minerals and rivers. And there's a boy
who comes here often whose face
and scalp are a tattoo wing, as if
a bird once worn as a hat has left
behind its shadow. When it's cold
he covers his wing with a red knit cap,
the face of Che Guevara embroidered
on one side. He's old enough to know
how his commitments have limited
his life. I try to remain astonished,
not condescending, though the truth is
I could love her whose bad choices
are a cost of fashion, who's wearing
this moment the latest boots from
New Zealand, and not him
who simply cares more than I do
about things neither of us can change.
I met her at a Christmas party the year
before it all came apart, a sort of
postmodern get-together, pepperoni rolls
and paté, Budweiser and Krug.
We talked about Reynolds Price
in the kitchen, smoking cigarettes
out the window above the sink.
She'd known Price at Duke, and as she
took the cigarette from my fingers,

she leaned in a little, as if to hear
a secret. Of course she was lovely,
and that's the problem—her boots
and her loveliness, an *awareness* of
her loveliness, which in West Virginia
can lead to a sense of privilege,
though such entitlement isn't
exclusive to Appalachia. Still,
beauty as a form of currency
has more value, one could argue,
where the common coin is uncommonly
rare, where so many are so damn poor.
The snow blew in the window,
so our hands shook a little as we
passed the cigarette back and forth.
I remember feeling awake in my body
in a way I'd never known when I turned
away from her to answer a question.
There was no one there, no one
waiting for an answer, and no one
anywhere when I turned back.

Your Favorite Things

I wish I could show you
this evening, the silver accidents
of lilac doused with shade,
the doves out of exile shining
on the wires, the last light. Early May
is a suburb's chance to be sentimental,
all the wounds half-healed,
the dogwood useless without
the snow shovel and salt
still tucked into a corner of the porch.
A rope hits the sidewalk
two blocks away, a girl's throat
filling with rhyme as she waits
for her sister to enter
the brief dwelling inscribed in air.
No fireflies yet. First corn
at the farmstands but no cantaloupe,
no watermelon. I wish
the bandages would fall from
the maple tree next door.
I wish the face in the privet
would turn away. And the blue vents
in an evening sky so close to
healing. And the friend in his
favorite suit so close to being healed.
I wish I could show you this evening,
the cufflinks glittering in the grass. No.
Here they are, the fireflies. Too soon.

Held Down

There goes the gravity.

And with it the light,
the savage little glow
at the edges of money, the smaller
sparks surrounding
wrapped packages, lettuce
in red rubber bands,
all the muttering into hands.
So much is stained when the light goes.
Now this walking around
on my fingertips.

Whenever I think about
thinking whenever I think
about it, the blue air of evening sticks
in my throat.
So I let the reeds whistle

to stillness.
And would the men
with their cameras, their miner's helmets,
could they all please extinguish
the little lamps? Not everyone

wants the silver prize. The dazed for instance.
The three or four shot full of holes.
The pears in honey.
Who do I ask about the pears in honey?

Let the reeds whistle to stillness.
Let the meadow burn with old moonlight,
the sticky tarnish lathering the leaves
and raining down the first cool night.

There goes
the gravity.
And a little boy too thin
for his cousin's old jeans
is released from the rules of standing still, of
listening without a word, all these
shadows breaking apart, the warped seconds
wrinkling the air like heat
above the tarmac, the boy rising,
a plastic sack inviting the wind,

falling back at last into
his body, his body blue
from the hands
tightening, holding him down.
Who do I ask?

Let the reeds whistle
like shells singing across a field,
like shells holding the wind
in their cheeks, ash instead of sand.

Who do I ask about this little earth?
(Which is all we have
and not enough.)

Now this walking around on my fingertips.

Let the reeds, the gravity, all this
light leaking into the dirt, the leaves, let it...
let the grass catch fire, the
celestial heat. It's traveled so far
to burn right through you. Let it.

Breakfast in West Virginia

Daylight at the end of the street.
The trees tipped with it.
Oatmeal in a yellow bowl. The roar
deep within the snow drifting along the fence.
Seven words for winter blend softly
in the mouth of the wind.
Cut back the roses. Cedar mulch
on the deep daffodils, deeper tulips.
Avenues along the river, the frozen verge,
barge shadows, old voices trapped
in the capped mines. Seven sounds for coal
piled by the tracks, heaped in open
boxcars, furred with frost. A box
of cereal and an empty bowl. Peeled
apple for Phoebe. Walt pours his own milk.
He wants to throw his toast in the snow,
"where the deer can find it." He has his face
against the window, can see the stain
of house lights on the dark yard, the last
stars in the western sky. A car door
slams, the paper hitting the porch. And then
nothing, as the children chew silently, snow
filling slowly every opening in the earth.

Like Mercury, the Monongahela

What did Sinclair Lewis say
about sweet potatoes, or rather
Upton Sinclair, or red potatoes?
Crows. Crows all day. And the river
holding onto the mist, sixty
watts of sunshine at noon
and the smell of cadmium
under the bridge, coal yards
and dumps, the boat launch south
of the locks, fission in a flock
of geese giving up on true
north, the slip toward Ohio, iron
buried along the river, in
backyards and vacant lots.
What did Andrew Carnegie say
or rather Jackson, or Webber?
Between Uniontown and Pittsburgh
there are seventeen places to buy
a burger. Behind the buildings
fronting Beechurst, the wooden
porches and stairways lean wildly
and crumble, concealing nothing
at last but neglect's abandoned
concealment. And further back
the river: no longer dead but
slow and empty of barges till
after midnight when the coal
in heaps is humped north: the river
flows north in a rhyme of night.
Warehouses into restaurants.
The sleek and soon-to-be sleek.
The furious pedaling beside
the abandoned tracks, C & O
so long, as gone as summer

in September, the heat hanging on
in spite of a blush spreading
from hollows to hillsides.
And the slick film of dust
on a working river, like ice
from a distance, a shiny gray,
like mercury. Ducks so full
of bread they leak as they run,
as they flee the town's mad chef,
out again before dawn to find
his menu. Found Food Fondue.
Wasn't it Charles Lindbergh
I mean Atlas god help us who
asked at the end of the day for
a salad, "Just a salad, thanks,"
then pointed out the last green
leaf on a sugar maple gone to ashes?

Comedy: Morgantown, West Virginia

Don Knotts Boulevard runs along the river
from the bridge to the locks
where it takes up its old name again until the highway.
There is nothing funny about comedy,
good comedy, since the cost
is regret at best, or loss, sometimes sadness:
the happy fool trails a ghost. And so
the street deserves its name, or rather, Knotts deserves
the honor, his humor
a sort of nocturne
to daylight, nonesuch
in a crowd.
There is an unnamed galaxy that puzzles
the physicists at Cal Tech
who dust their hair with chalk to get closer to
the old ways, those days
when thinking was an event within slate-
covered walls, the windows
open to jasmine and orange blossoms, the percolating clouds
of diesel and car exhaust. They made
theorems and stood around
listening to the light, all that bruise
and shuffle.
On warm evenings
after afternoons around the pool
which followed mornings in the classrooms, a group of laureates
in straw hats drank
rum and San Miguel, drummed for hours in a circle waiting
for sweet deliverance
and slow stars,
which is why it surprised them: to see a wash
of dust harden into
light, the galaxy closer than any other but never noticed
for its filth, its slow-
dissolving heat, the cold years it took to get here.
There are no theories of laughter that don't end

at the door; there is nothing
to know in the friendly talk around pools
and card tables, the poker game alfresco
on a warm California night when all
that's said is a way of closing off
the possibility of sadness in the summer sky:
the unseen, the unnamed, the unknown.
"So anyway," someone says.
"How many physicists does it take..."
and all else including light is buried or burned into nothing.
Though matter remains.
Like laughter
in a blue glow after midnight
when everyone else
is asleep, the hum of traffic
on the boulevard.
A rerun of *Andy Griffith* sizzles off through the atmosphere:
it will be understood
or not when it's finally cleaned
from the dust of the cosmos
and played again to the unsuspecting
and unimagined, or just to the last of us so many
years from now, somehow lost on our way home.

Nothing New but Everything

"O, Lord love me," I heard someone say. I heard the glass
settle in a shoe, the secession
of sparrows, the smoke swallowed like a cup of soup. I heard
once that a boy in a blue hat
is a pinhole of sky in the summer grass—
if seen from a satellite, from a nest feathered with thistledown,
with dust. O finger of ash in an old shell.
O love me sweet air at the end
of a plea. A while ago
the silver and the light left a snapshot squared
by deliberated purpose:
by love or hope or reckless faith in the everafter. And now.
I heard a whistle in the tiled tunnel. I heard O
who knows how cautiously we care
for the sounds beneath the sounds, for faces
framed by newsprint, for prayers like small sails loose in the wind.

Tribe and Country

Pre-dawn sonatas, the lowing in a far-off field.
Trash cans inspected, their lids replaced,
the shambling off, the tired and befuddled

who dream in daylight of swimming pools and beer,
flecks of ash in their hair, the singed sky.
Through the streets the sheep are herded

from hills beyond the projects to fenced yards
and birthing pens. A clock through a window,
an empty coat by the door. And now the animating

light of day. Children invented. Their moans,
their brown shoes. A shiver of traffic
over stones and cracked pavement, a lamppost

becomes a vendor; he builds a kiosk out of leaves.
From a small girl's neck, a red scarf is torn;
she is sent home, the scarf buried, the buses ...

the buses collect commuters, who face each other's hair
or read the advertisements for tonics and fraternity:
exact change or a token, a smile, a nod.

The stoplight drops into the street and rolls
away. A man renounces his class, removes his hat
and climbs the pole to take its place yelling,

go, get ready, stop, a steady job. Mounting the steps
the governor, faces the cameras, ungloves
his hands. *Full employment at last,* he says,

even as the signalman remembers his baldness,
clutches for his hat, which isn't there, tumbles
into traffic. If he is killed, says a journalist,

the statistics will stay the same. A small woman
surprises herself by screaming. She had meant to yawn.

Landscape as the Latest Diet (Southern California)

Instead of butter, the ten a.m. light of June
    on Little Island, masts blending the mist
      until it clarifies into nothing.

Instead of salt, the sand beneath
    Balboa pier, cool even in July, trimmed
    with wrack and empty cans, the blue haze of spray
    and breeze between the pilings.

Instead of bread, the violet stains
    on the sidewalks of South Pasadena, the jacarandas,
      their small cry tuned to rhyme the sky.

Instead of eggs, the foothills under smog, the sage
    and scrub oak browned by drought
    and the tick of ozone in the air.

Instead of meat, the arroyo at sunrise, the gray
    inside gray of tulle fog and
    coyote, coyote bouncing down
    the deer trail, a pigeon in its mouth.

Instead of sugar, the date palms along
    the dry wash gathering wind
    in their fronds for the hourly reprimand,
    an endless hush.

Instead of wine, the smell of oranges
    and ocean water, the smoke
    of smudge pots before dawn.

Instead of supper, the song of bells
    in the harbor, the seals draped
    over buoys like fat uncles on the furniture.

And everyone at ease in the middle distance, in repose.
　And the meal, like memory, a cure
　　for nothing but hunger, but forgetting.

If I Could Break Down Anywhere it Would Be Halfway to Todos Santos,

which seems safely far away, long ago,
vaguely placed and indeterminate.

I could name a village but then I'd know
where I'm driving to these days.

At the hospital yesterday, a handful
of flowers for Gloria,
                            something to place
in a vase next to the jar holding her
appendix, halfway across the parking lot

I thought, "Is she right?" and I wasn't
thinking of Gloria anymore, self-absorbed
as always,
              as everyone, just standing
there beneath the haze worrying about
blame, wishing for
                        blamelessness (as if
the beautiful really are),
sweating all over in the lousy lung of July,
just standing in my juices wondering

how wrong it can get before the toaster talks
back to the bread so to speak, until
the itch spreads inside
                              and you're scratching
the back of your head so to speak, trying
to reach that spot behind the eyes.

I didn't go to Rome to sit and wait
on the Spanish Steps for someone I haven't
seen in years to wander by,
                              to give it all away

to fate, to do my best John Keats (*"Please* put
your scarf on") while no one
wondered where I'd gotten to.

Halfway to Todos Santos I broke down
in a Reagan-era Ford and took cover
at a cantina overlooking the Pacific:
slender breeze, thatched roof, beer named
for the view.
        I didn't drink and drink
and drink for days though I thought about it;
I found a guy who knew Fords and moved on
to Todos Santos,
           where Tom and Jeff and Sal
were waiting, glasses of gold tequila
in ranks on the bar.
          By breakdown I mean
something different these days, that charming
stammer that turns into
          one long sentence
under the sun, one sentence of one phrase
done over and over until good and cooked,

until a hand guides you toward the doors
and you hear your own voice say,
"Can you give these to Gloria?"
And another voice says, "*Otra vez?*"

And I answer, "*Sí. Uno más,
uno Pacifico.*" But it's too late for that.
And someone says,
        "He's speaking Spanish,"
but she isn't talking to me, doesn't hear me ask
"How far is it to Todos Santos?" doesn't point
at the sea,
       which is south of us somehow

and swallowing the sun like an aspirin,
doesn't say, "Why you're halfway there."

And then it's July in West Virginia.
And someone gives me water. And he says,
"It's just the heat, it's really hot,"
                                        but it isn't.
The water's cool, like the waves at Todos Santos,
the deep ocean currents heading for Alaska,

the way each day ends with a drowning
so to speak,
              with a line of friends toasting
the darkness, though they're facing
the other way, toward the sea, where the sun
has gone again: a splash of fire, a sizzle, gone.

The water's cool and I drink it in, drink it down
to silence, to nothing so to speak.
                                        Nothing.

But that was yesterday. I'm on my way today
to Todos Santos, to Todos Santos, to Todos Santos.

Mountaintop Removal, Wallace Stevens, My Son Walt, West Virginia

Light the way, the old miner said. When we
turned around even the darkness was gone.
Walt finds the k from the broken keyboard, sings
down the stairs, *for kisses, for koala, for king, for
could be could be,* oh no, (he's never heard of
the letter C) *for cowboys, for kites, for
Kevin, for continent,* the edges crumbling *for crumbs*
into the sea, all of us and everything *for care,* take care,
*for Carrie, for candy, for kettle, for cookie, for kids,
for coal,* each end of the chain hooked to a backhoe
and Drive, she said, she said I'm sick of it, just drive
for light, *for car, for country, for king, for* Oh he said, *I
said that,* he laughs, he's laughing, Walt owns the *k,*
he's king. A kind of Cardinal. So light the first
light, as if as if as if *for coal, for keys and keyholes, for
care, for taking care,* take care, *for cap and coal
and capped coal mines, for King Walt, King Coal,*
the blue light above the aisle of evening, of dwellings
in the evening air, in mountainsides sealed from
without, roots of hardwood twined with miners,
their ghosts, even the darkness gone, *for kin, for cousins,
for carrying on.* It's never enough. Just being here.

She Said

Sometimes it overtakes me.
Sometimes we're overtaken.
Silver in the salt and pepper.
Hands creased with fortunes withheld.
Hold on, she said. Just wait.
She sorted photographs like playing cards.
She drew a hand to her chest.
Sometimes it seems the forest
beyond the yard is holding daylight
in its teeth. The night, she said.
It's losing its little shine.
She's left the door open. And now
the wind, with its retinue of ash and
litter, those chips of light lodging
and dislodging ... no one knows
how sanded down by light
we've become. You'll be safe here,
she said, drawing close her burlap
shawl, sighting low along the barrel.
Beyond the field's ragged edge
the war was over, though as always
the news of such things turned
to weather: through smoke
or snow, the broadcast day begins.
She said, Here you are with more hair.
Here's the sky, the sea, the spire
at San Ramon. Oh, I see, she said.
That isn't you at all. I see.

Elegy by Frank Gehry

The Corcoran Gallery, Washington, DC

I wasn't sure what to do.
At the Safeway on Pico I built
your favorite meal from the inside out,
piled it all in the shopping cart:
olive oil and chicken broth, tomatoes,
green peppers, an onion and a pound
of shrimp, a half-pound each of squid,
swordfish and halibut, a whole chicken and
all of the above except oil and broth
cut into small pieces, though I never
got that far, a pound of mussels, a lemon,
three cups of short grain rice, garlic, parsley,
salt and saffron... I brought it all home.
And there on the kitchen counters
I made your meal, the boxes and bags,
the vegetables, vials of spices,
a small junkyard of mussels, the curls
of shrimp lined like a sentence of commas
along the edge of the drainboard,
two saucepans and a kettle held ajar
by wooden spoons, stainless tents
on a plain of white Formica.
When Berta arrived home the kitchen
stank of rotten ocean critters.
I couldn't cook it: your favorite meal.
Between the war and your last abstraction
(a field of wheat, a river and two feet
of sky), the story of your life, of a boy
broken hard on his father's knee,
bulged and folded in, like a twist
of bunting blown two ways at once.
I wanted to build that story, hold it

in place. So I looked for a crack where all
the used light leaks in, where you made
your art. And there, between a reliquary
of office machinery and the last good idea
in DC, I built you. Forgive me. Forever
you'll listen to the pitiable, endless evasions
of senators and diplomats, the small-
minded legislators eating lunch from
paper sacks while walking their twenty
minutes on the Mall. But one window
is enough. Through it the eternal
agents of history will stare at flecks of time
scattered like wreckage through the rooms,
rooms so white and otherwise vacant
no one will think to look up.
I'll build you into the emptiness above,
as once, in the cathedrals of Europe, space
was left for the angels, who never rest.

TWO

After West

After West

After west when every bit of it
was used and torn and blessed anyway, when every
mind changed and there wasn't room
for every changed mind, when
the backyard logic and the dry, stone birdbaths
and the dust on every wing—the leaf dust and diesel dust
and powder dusted in the whorls of abandoned fingerprints—
when everyone after west
stood with their backs to the boiling ocean
waiting to be overcome, when no one
worried, grew weary, woke wondering where
in the world anymore, for any reason
other than there wasn't any west, any way
to grow the new idea
though after west there was a new west
without veins in the riverbeds or mine shafts or valleys
so thick with loam
the rice grew alongside the almond trees,
a new west of mist and morning haze, a west
inside the clouds slowly dissolving
to sea, a nest no west for the weightless infidels,
the transubstantiated and transported,
those changed already into light and light
enough to float free and loose just
west of west, where no one needed west
though they needed everything else.

After west the smoke
softened the sharp air and settled
into valleys, the wide arroyos, the waves
gray between the crests, ash filling
the open eyes. We closed
all eyes, we walked and we did it.

We walked below Wilshire
just closing every eye.

———※———

After west was gold: the poppies
gold, the eagles gold, the sage dry
and yellow and going gold, the wrecked
foothills north and east all blotched
with it and burning, the faithless
sands beneath the clay, the backyards of
West, of Toluca Lake and Hancock Park
and Bel Air and Pacific Palisades and
West Hollywood, Westwood,
West Los Angeles, Western Boulevard.
West is west is gold.

———※———

There were once two wests
before 1968, the west of Hughes
and Hollywood, the west of Chavez
and Bobby Kennedy. After west
there were two hundred known wests
named nightly on the stoops
of East Los Angeles, the doorways of
Little Tokyo, Little Saigon, the streets
of Compton, Dorsey Avenue, Farmers
Market on Fairfax, the stables
at the far end of the valley, all west of
Barstow and Phoenix and Victorville and
slipping like secrets drifting into rumors,
slipping west into the sea.

———※———

After west a pissed-off baby boy
slugs the midwife on his way to
his mother's breast, too much time
in the hot entryway to all this light,
these foolish grins. But now
the west is unknowable, a pink
fist thumping high on the chest
to let the milk down, striated light
in yellow-to-orange scales above
a broken, gray Pacific, a line
of boys, no, men, walking the rail
at the end of the pier, now dropping
like bits of laughter, torn laughter,
into the wave just beginning to feel
its height, just beginning to crest
as a body enters from above.

Walt arrives after west
with a small branch stripped of leaves
and a half-chewed bone he's found
under the rhododendron, this wild
incompletion Lynda talked about,
two coughs after midnight and
a domelight recovering the cupped space
inside a hand, Walt awake after west,
long after he promised his own
little god behind the rocking horse
he'd be asleep, safe in dreams
of dogs and monkeys.

41

(after Machado)

After west we will see your face
in the dark hole in the afternoon, a day
torn to smoke by passing storms
and flapping senselessly like
frayed sunlight. Dune grass
under water, the train stopped short
of San Clemente, a sudden mudslide,
the tracks in tangles. Entrained to
Coronado, the passengers forced now
to disembark, nudged and urged,
herded gently like blind salmon in
a covered aqueduct to buses as evening
rushes from the arroyo. The Pacific
rain is news from the west. Yellow
ponchos for the elderly, the thermoses
of coffee, the free oranges and small boxes
of old raisins. She chews the dried
fruit and sings; he sips and spills
the thin coffee. Orange peels now
in the sudden moonlight scattered
on the tracks. Next stop
but who's to say where south begins
when Oceanside is after west, when
San Diego is after west, Tijuana
after west, the frontier is after west,
is Baja and the Sea of California:
Here's the end of it, said Cortez,
At last we see it, said Balboa: the west
Atlantic, so gently blue.

After west the colors changed but not
the words, though they slid a little,
like plates of earth. And at the edges: west:
the water so clear and calm;
the dune so blind and blind. And there we were,
the continental shelf. Near the top
the white bushes of volcanic rock,
the green-black of trees of kelp.
The prismatic sway of hanging jellyfish, the clear
silver, the opalescence of light behind flesh.
The window stillness of climbing birds.
The yellow-pink-lilac of fish taking flight.
The orange-lavender-lily of doves hunkering down
on floating timbers, on wrack and litter.
And at the foot of the waxy seaweed the azure foot
of an old pelican.
And at the head of the stone-still palms, the red
sea cucumbers and urchins green and purple,
at the head of it all the west,
a sun titrating sea. Desert flowers and the yucca,
from a distance, from west, so brown they're almost
yellow, gold again, it's all gold.

—⚹—

(Pastoral by Frank Gehry)

Panama Museum of Biodiversity

After west the galvanized nails
and sheep. The corrugated cardboard
rolled into shade beneath tin trees
or leaves like curled shavings
in the lee of a rusty knoll.
And the quietest little robot boy,
arms in pieces on the factory
floor of afternoon in the far field,
his flock as scattered as wind-up
sparrows ... O, robot boy with
no way to hold the nothing
left to hold, lie down and sleep.
All told the ashen sky breaks
twice each night: to let in
the electric moon, to let it out,
though every other minute
the halogen burns those bits
of air left over, this small dome
of glass fogging up with old
breath, this little Earth below,
so ragged and used. The silver
stream slows to quicksilver,
to liquid lead, the long mirror.
And the far field fills with shattered
glass, a thousand years of broken
wine bottles spread carefully
on the meadow, green on green,
light roaring in all the in-between.
Robot boy would dream of singing
to his sheep, of hooking fingers
in thick wool, if anything so tired

and wrecked, so filled with circuitry
and grief could really dream.
Sleep, my robot boy, and wake
to a world as empty of anything
as you. By then your arms
will be ready, repaired and
reattached. The dreamless
reinvent themselves each morning—
they find the strength to take
whatever at all in their arms,
to comfort the near at hand.
Those without hope are nearly
as able, though each night
they are forced to dream.
Therein lies the difference
between my robot boy and me.

After west was five a.m.
The submarine arrives in the harbor locked shut
for weeks by ice. After west
was ice. No one climbs from
the periscope tower; no eye looks out
at the shipyard stunned to silence
by a new moon. In the dark diner
on the pier, the pies at rest
beneath glass find the one shaft of
street light and glow like useless
brains awaiting dissection.
A police car idles in the steam and smoke,
a hand at the end of a cigarette, draped
from a half-rolled-away window.

And now the horizon at sea, a reflected
pink, and above a vanished sea a cloud cracks
as if to release a flock of gulls, a slant
of sunlight, a little air
into this picture.

—*—

O, west the blue thought
imagined by plains so racked
by dust-wind, by light.

—*—

In Laurel Canyon
after west, the tribes, their rope sandals
and seashell shards glazing
the wall-tops, the ad hoc
love in slipstream trailers
trembling in the aftershocks,
a dry wash remembering rock, remembering
mountains and sky and sky
lying down in the river,
oh, yes, the river—
sweet doppelgänger, sweet sluice
as sure as a diamond bit,
the buckets of dust
dragged home to bathe
the babies of the new age,
since all is aftermath,
after west.

—*—

After all, after changes,
after secrets, after her,
after wonder, after dolor,
after long, after her,
after leaving, after staying,
after getting used to her,
after honor, after sickness,
after health, after her,
after knowing, after noon,
after getting over her,
after naps in late morning,
after sweetness, after her,
after keeping, after waking
into evenings after her,
after ruin, after roses,
after all there was in her,
ever after there's an after,
after west is after her.

After Walt, after west:
Phoebe, swift letter from Thebes
delivered by wings
after midnight, tucked between
tail feathers, the garden stones
tipped over, who's never seen
Pacifica, lost land beneath the tide,
and even now the west
is waiting: ever after, even now.

After we lost the west
the sand shook into water and the water,
we lost the water and the old words, the old
ways, the old ones walking too close
to the sea, to the highway. We lost
the saddles strapped to the lost gelding,
we lost the dapples, we lost the grays.
We lost our maps, we lost our legends,
we lost the compass point spinning west
as if the west were a filing buried
in the beach, we could almost see it,
almost west: after west
was everything else.

THREE

And when I thought,
"Our love might end"
the sun
went right on shining

–James Schuyler

Love Poem by Frank Gehry

The Weisman Museum, Minneapolis

When I remember you now, your face
is a silver smear, a river curling in a winter sky.
Or yesterday, as dusk leaked from idea into orange,
your face again: a swift mirror in the earth, all spin
and yellow friction, the sky's harbor of foil
and strips of tin, a beer can torn to shreds, fugue
of sails in a singing sunshine.

One day,
many years ago in California, your face turned into
a kite and fell beside the river, river torn from
the sea, my long knife near Ocean Park, silver scissors
in the blue. *Richard, you old square*, I remember saying
as I took apart the cigar box, wet the wood and let it warp
in the damp heat near his studio. When blue is bent
it turns to sky. The opposite of gray is gray. And every ounce
of steel in a wall above the river can't hold
the light of your eyes slowly turning to lead in memory.
Who said, Love is the price of love?

Well, I thank them.
When I remember you now your face has the petty hope
of a scar beneath makeup. And beneath every roof, inside every
wall holding out the dumb truths is a room we could spend
our lives inside. But something wants us where it can see us.
And for that it invented beauty, for which we rush
outside to see, looking back all the while at what held us.
What held us? Architecture is an afterthought of purpose
in love with its mistakes, its limits. How I loved you.

A Friday at the End of August

At the northern end of the valley they're shaking
the almond trees again. My mother's teeth

begin to ache about five, just as the tractors
retract their mechanical arms and let go
of the trunks. Then she hears what's been lost

all afternoon: the stolen song of a sole
mockingbird nesting in a fence post, the pool sweep

hissing as it plunges and cleans, Gene in the garage
sawing boards for a new bureau. And beneath
the dull whine, the trill and sizzle, a fleck of voice

gathers with the wet music from a pocket radio, a word
or two she remembers from her years along the border,

the shavings of Spanish chipping the dusty air
at the end of the street, where she knows, since
her fillings hurt, since the workday is settling

with blown dirt in the orchard beyond
the cul-de-sac, where she knows a half-dozen

migrant workers, what her father-in-law called
"wetbacks," are singing with their wine, their cold
pink wine hidden for hours in the mud of

an aqueduct and now unburied, uncorked,
the mockingbird trying to get it right, this new

song, new words arriving in pieces, *solamente
una vez, no más*, the bones of language hung
as always with laughter, with music, so many almonds

drying in the dirt beneath the trees, the tractor parked
at the end of the last row, a smudge pot and

a litter of cards, the lost deck from last Friday.
My mother walks out on the patio to sing along,
the oleander's blue shade softening the heat—she knows

the words, remembers a cantina above the river.
And here's Gene with a glass of good Modesto wine,

nothing fancy but cold, the pool in shadow, the day
retreating, a blade of light dulled by now, the last cut
deep and wet in the blue-black Pacific. "How about a swim?"

Gene says, his voice amid song and silence, his voice
and all the others, the border music, the psalm of evening.

As If

Across the street he took your hand
as if lifting a length of fabric, as if to test its loveliness, held it
    lightly
as if he planned to let it go, feel the cool slither of fingers
    trailing his palm,
as if the vaguest breeze could flutter your hand back into his,
as if all this life and part of others he'd handled the finest bolts
of cloth, held them high for kings and queens to esteem,
as if beauty were his coin and currency, though I could see
it wasn't his to have, wasn't any more the point
than air is the point of breathing,
that you'd let your hand be held without
giving anything away.

And instead of hoping I slipped back
into the coffee shop and waited by the window for you
to walk away. As if I cared. As if I saw at last
what you looked like in the hat I bought
last fall, the gloves you said were perfect.
As if across the street you stood
with someone else waiting
for the light to change.
What else to do while waiting?
He took your hand.
Take it back.

Our Fathers

So we'll never hear Sinatra
the way our fathers did, who wander the rooms
in their pajamas wondering where in the world,
where? And someone says, No,
no thank you, sick of listening to strangers
in the street, sick of coming home in doubt
or in time for the familiar meal, the usual
complaints, fingers extended as the polish dries.
Our fathers. Alone or together alone
with the new wives that never took.
And the coffee by the window. And the neighbor's
dogs chasing deer down the driveway.
The arrival of mail and the afternoon light, a bruise
in the birches crowding the house.
Our fathers, for whom the days cannot pass
slowly enough, who find their old hats
behind the shoe boxes and photo albums
and say, Why not? For Frank before Las Vegas,
for DiMaggio and Bogart. They say, The evening
is wider than a mile, though of course nothing
is waiting on the other side,
nothing but night.

Knowing You Were Loved

What is it about the reeds, the muddy fields, those voices
no one else would love? How long
will I wait to start pretending again? These months
outside my body have felt a little like
the shivering of a boy at the edge of the sea, who looks back
at the waves with a longing so pure
it is, perhaps, the only moment in his life he'll truly wish
to die. Suicide is wisdom at default.
The boy is past that—he wants to be cold again, just
tumbling in the surf, not postponing life, not avoiding
anything, though at any moment I will not reenter
my body. "Like priests," you said, "we do nothing
the best we can." But you were waiting in the half-light
before dawn, sitting alone at the window
as your husband and child slept ... no. You were flaking
candle wax with a fingernail, the planes
passing overhead. You were listening for matins
as the merchants unloaded their wagons.
So now you're a voice in the reeds and all I do is hear you.
I don't want to lie again. I'm tired of lying.
But there it is, my body, waiting.

Days

Instead of Wednesday the blue lawn before sunrise explained a lot of things but not that, not Wednesday. Just dew and late stars, less light than noon and who knows about Friday. What with soandso prescribing rain from the blue room, what with someonewhoknewyou saying it's sad isn't it? But it isn't. It isn't sad or silver-smoky-grey or once-wounded, though once the wounded knew enough to breathe through the vents in their chests, the billows instead of lungs but never gills, not that. Not that not ever. And never Tuesday. I mean who knew? Tuesday the neighbor's cat ran through the petunias, found a crack in the air and vanished into Monday. She won't be missed. Sad is Sunday night, the fossil fingerprint of school figures, someone lost on the ice beyond rubber cones dusted with snow. Siegfried Sassoon: there, I've said it; he found a poplar fat enough to hide behind, which leaves us Thursday, no, Saturday. There's no pulse in the neck of Thursday, and the whole town's on its way to Saturday, skid marks on the arms of someone so shattered by lemonade on the porch she's singing, she's leaning into the last turn, into Saturday. Always Saturday.

Phoebe at Daybreak

A cricket behind the refrigerator.

Or the dull-eyed neighbor at dawn

dragging her vacuum cleaner down
the sidewalk after leaves, singing to
no one or a cat that watches from the porch.

Two blocks to Pleasant Street. Thirty-two
miles to Friendsville. Phoebe

at daybreak crawling from the corner,
waving board books and singing, just

"semaphore and gibberish," or so sayeth
Elvis Costello (né Declan MacManus), King

of America. *Decisions in moonlight
are delights in the day.*
And after lo mein and General Tso's

chicken, OK. Believe me, believe me,
believe me, sings the cricket. But it's
dawn, so a small thrush is just
holding on to the night. O, nightingale

in darkness, I present you my Phoebe,
my flycatcher, my moonlight over suburbs
too sad to know their own sweetness.

When Dean Left West Virginia

When Dean left I took the kids
to the Toys 'R' Us off Moon Parkway
and said, Whatever you want (Dean
had given me a twenty to spend on them)
knowing their tastes run to things
they can hold in one hand.
It occurred to me that nothing much
happened in West Virginia prior
to Keats' birth but since then, whew:
every damn tree and nearly all
the mountaintops: "Whoosh,"
says Todd from Mingo County.
"What's that?" "The sound of
a mountain being shaved down to size."
Coal juice and slag. The rivers
silting in like a fat man's arteries.
Dolly Sods, where red spruce and
hemlock needled the clouds
now almost lunar but lovely, an un-
exploded mortar shell every
now and then unburied by the wind
(DON'T TOUCH, say the Guidebooks),
a land like the hilltops of southwestern
France, the DMZ or some other place
it all went down. Phoebe bought a plush dog
and named her Kelly. Walt
couldn't find a thing, though later
at the Wal★Mart bought a Scooby-Doo
video for nine dollars plus tax.
We all watched it twice waiting
for Mom to come home. "Whoosh,"
says Walt. "What's that?" "That's
Scooby turning into smoke."

Spring in Lincoln Park, 1910

If I were Edgar Alwin Payne in 1910 in Chicago
it wouldn't be spring. Late autumn perhaps, knowing who
I am today, what is happening to me and because of me.
In autumn the distant trees are russet as they say, nearly red.
In autumn, the yellows so close to green in Payne
are leaning into gold.
                          It's not even Lincoln Park, not 1910.
I'm sick of 1910. What did they know of anything then?
Payne lived through 1917, through '29 and '39 painting
landscapes in California, a plein-air Catastrophist.
Who had he lost to lay the shadows so deeply
in the lake, to put them in the water and beneath it,
as if lake water, really, is another form of shadow?
And how did the sky fall so far,
                          leave its stains on the grass
where leaves would linger in autumn, the ground wet
and muddy, the smeared brown so nearly gray.
Still, his clouds are right.
                  He has them wrong
for spring—they are low and loaded, weighing down
the yellow trees like a theme, the idea of loss, which today
I've washed from my hands and face, slamming
the medicine cabinet door open against the wall;
I don't want to see you, Edgar Payne.
                   It is nearing dusk
in your painting, the buried pink in one corner: day's end
as pentimento. Well, it's morning here. Clouds stand in ranks
in the eastern sky. By afternoon it will rain. Did my son
hear the fleck of Payne's gray (William not Edgar)
in my voice over breakfast.
                Could he feel, at seven,
the heavy brush stroke, my admission not to him
or his mother or anyone anywhere in the living world
that if it were up to me....
                 I'm painting the sky, Edgar Payne,
filling the spaces between clouds. By afternoon it will rain.

February

A magnifying glass, two poker chips
and a plastic dinosaur in his pocket, Walt
falls asleep mid-chew, leaves the rest
of his bologna to the charity of winter,
its thrifty hours south of noon.
Carnations the color of plums, the daisies
gone first, petals floating in the vase water.
February in West Virginia, sunlight
through windows buttering
the pine floors, a basket of warm clothes
to fold, Phoebe naming them: *blue sock,*
pretty dress, blue sock, every shirt a sort of
hat. At five o'clock the postman rings to let us
know he's late. And the light seems to sizzle
as it settles into shadows, at the edges of which
something moves. Something always moves.

Isn't That Enough

Describe the late evening light without
saying what it means to you
and all allowances of hope and faith
and the gentle loneliness will vanish
like variables in a long-solved problem,
though there's a problem with settling for verbs about
absence, all that draining away, the insubstantial sifting.
I have a feeling it's time to gather up
the children and tell them everything, all that for years
we couldn't say, most of which has to do
with the vast retreating afternoon. No one's
avoiding life; no one is ignoring the plans
we made for each other: the small graveyard
near the river behind Pisgah Church,
where the kids leaned against the stones and ate
their sandwiches while no one except you
rubbed dates onto paper and cried out
the names, the way the spellings had changed.
Eternity is the hardest bargain. I should've known
when you said you no longer cared where
you laid or with whom that things between us
had expanded: too much nothing. We all know
it's a lie, that bones don't reach across the space
between graves, no holding hands in the next life.
But it was a choice about *this* life, and now
it's been taken back. We wondered a bit when
your grandfather bought plots for everyone.
But if no one believes in loneliness beyond life,
then he'll lie there forever, little box of ash, and wait
to hear the news you promised to deliver:
that everyone's fine without him, just give us
some time, we'll be there soon. I want to be buried
where the kids can find me if they ever need to look.
Chances are they won't. But believe me, I'll wait.

An Accordion in Autumn

Is it coincidence? I know everyone
wonders what I wonder about
beauty: are we hard-wired to swoon
when the trees surprise us, as earlier
today I waited for Walt on the playground
and turned to watch the hills hold
the sun in their hollows, the yellow
rusting to orange in the dull wind
of a spinning earth? This close to the end
of October it's all murmur and centrifuge,
a chance to challenge the catalog
colorists, naming the red sweater "bruise
of apple," the gray jacket "doe at dawn."
And here's Walt, leaves in his hair: "boy as fawn."

For Ashes, For Letting Go

When will it stop, the slip
and cinder, salt staining
the brick stairs, complaints
yellowing the air at each edge
of breath? When will
the broken back heal into rain,
into heat beneath the earth, the grass,
its shimmer and ache?
April galleons in late March
scudding the pale blue
between trees. The whack
of sandals on paving stones.
For some, each day is a trick,
a joke whispered in the wake
of trains leaving. For some,
as we know, everything
will go wrong twice.
And the phone hidden
in the stove. The trembling.
So no one cares enough,
travels properly, the coach
and station. And with every meal
the fork, the knife, the useless
spoon. The last course is radicchio
and green leaf, a stain
of port over cracked lipstick.
For some it is not enough
to wake from the twin dreams
of wolves and feathered dogs.
And then the rest who never
sleep, never say anything like
I'm sorry, so long, does it hurt.

Everything is Given to Be Taken Away

to Peter Milton Walsh

There's nothing silver about it, holding on
as a sort of shine, seawater
in a vase. Let's limit the molecules, stand so close
in the surf we tear the ocean in two.
In time we'll join
a group for sandwiches and tea, still life
on the promontory, the tables
and plastic chairs all arranged in open air
in time as they say, in time
to watch the whales pass, the calves
nudging in the noisy mist
while a docent drones on, "The right whale
to hunt, the Southern Right:
slow swimmers, they float when slain."
Who wouldn't look away?
Who wouldn't wish to slap him? All this glass
and burnish we call light,
this way of cupping wind in two hands
like a drink. Ben Johnson lost
his first son though I don't know how:
"Farewell, thou child
of my right hand, and joy ... Seven years
thou wert lent to me,
and I thee pay...." Even then you couldn't
safely duel another man to death,
though Johnson did. But why and with what
I don't know. Then again,
hubris and a pistol, wine and the debt of words.
How could anyone lose so much and wake to wonder
if somewhere near a plate of toast

is steaming, the juice that tastes vaguely of soap.
My son is sleeping off an afternoon
of steady joy, pillowed deeply by an open book,
a wand in one fist. Someone
help me for imagining another's loss who lit
the pitcher of ocean water
a lavender of evenings, whose voice
sang the sweet terror of saying over and over
so long. So long.
A *life full of farewells*, none so final and silencing
as a child's.

If Afternoon

If afternoon and its narrow strips,
its ancient wallpaper of daylight slips
like a bandage from the trees;

if the barn swallows
mistake the shadows in the lee of the church
next door for the deeper silence
of chimneys;

if the last bee of summer
stings the windowpane
instead of the punished little boy,
housebound and devastated;

if the little boy dreams of wearing
a red jacket, if his
dreams near morning
flare and smoke, the film on fire;

if the neighbor's arthritic calico
drops like a weighted hook from the garden wall,
rolls twice in the grass and rights itself;

if anything at all is visible of noon's sheer edges;

if each sleeve and gloveful has been emptied;

if there is one note of yellow light in the legs of a cricket,
if it lodges in the air around your hands;

if afternoon lingers, if it stains
your clothes like pale dust lifted
by the wind,

if the second chance of evening
fails to bury the day;

if a hand so big it blackens the sky
can't hold this little earth safe a while in darkness;

if nothing else works, then and only then.

The Difficult Science of Separation

Fission in its original form, its first mission
held only that a thing could be itself

twice, though later (who knew?) the size
of selves began to shrink, as if the elves

we found beneath garden stones measuring the pounds
of thistledown and baling it for winter stuffing, the whistle

at dusk to call home the dogs—as if all of it were a way to ask
how we'd come so far from childhood just to find that now

atoms had run away with hope, our faith a thousand phantoms,
the cloud concealing sunset as toxic as the word *divorce* said
     aloud

while the children break apart their board books and smile,
as though a thing broken is really two things: one to love,
     one to know.

My Dream of Bob Marley

For years I've put the end at the end,
as if what he said meant something more
for coming so close to silence. But silence
was the point, two quiet streams heading
down the mountain through jungles so empty
the trees held the wind in their leaves just to
hear a sound like whispers, as if nature,
when it comes right down to it, misses us
as we will miss it some day. But it
was a dream: dream jungle, dream wind,
dream dog, dream Marley.

When Walt wishes for a dog
he describes an animal part alligator
and part sheep, with feathers like
a peacock and eyes the same color
as his sister's: a blue bordering on
sapphire, a blue so deep you know
she'll be trouble in fifteen years.
He will call this dog Blue after
the cartoon on television (not
the eyes), though I suggest Yellow
after a movie he's never seen.
But Walt says, No. Blue.

I woke from the dream four mornings
in a row and each morning was a dream itself:
January skies as blue as an old woman's
hair, the strangely warm breezes blowing up
my neck like the breath preceding a kiss.
In the clearing in the dream, he tended
the fire and boiled water in a beaten pan.

My father raised collies as a boy.
One of them appeared on the front
of a cereal box for saving a child
from a rattlesnake. With fame now
out of the question—used up by his
favorite dog—and bravery just as
unlikely, my father became
an Episcopal minister and left
at sunup each morning to write
sermons or jog or visit the hospitals
before his office hours began at nine.
My mother, over breakfast, never told
us her dreams, just that they started
at dawn and stopped when one of us
called out for help in the bathroom.

When the dog enters the campsite,
trotting with purpose, as most starving
animals do, a dog so filthy it threatens
to make the air unbreathable, the dust
rising off its coat like steam from a wet
horse in winter, when the dog finally
makes its appearance, Bob Marley looks up
from the fire he's prodding with a leafy stick.
And here's the end, helplessly last, as usual:
Marley points the burning branch at the dog,
sitting now at the edge of the clearing.
"You must wash that white dog," he says.
And I wake up. I understand the dog, and
what it means that I should wash it. But
why Marley? My friend Lou says I should
be glad it's not Wayne Newtown and go back
to bed. But what would Wayne be doing
in a jungle? And why the leaves, why
the fire? My wife says, "You're just hungry,
go to sleep." And that makes sense.

Phoebe is convinced that spinach
is a type of yogurt, and she will
sing in her highchair with spinach
in her hair and in her ears and up
her nose until the last pureed drip
of it falls into her lap. "Yogurt,"
she will say, as if naming the meal
now that it's gone will change its
chemistry or its reputation, will
sweeten the very soil in which it's grown.

But I'm not hungry. I think I dream of
Bob Marley because he is so irretrievably
gone. And no matter how hard I scrub,
that dog is never coming clean, never changing
back to what I can't see in the dream:
a white dog with a rattlesnake in his teeth,
hungrier than I will ever be, and just a dream.
Phoebe sleeps on into the named night,
her brother across the room; there is no bravery
in the world enough to ensure anything.

Notes

The italicized passages in "After West" section eight were inadvertently borrowed from Blaise Cendrars: the unconscious is a thief.

The following poems were inspired by and in some cases take their titles from songs by Peter Milton Walsh, who for many years led a band called The Apartments: "Everything is Given to Be Taken Away," "If I Could Break Down Anywhere it Would Be Halfway to Todos Santos," "Our Fathers," "Knowing You Were Loved."

"On Beauty and West Virginia at the Blue Moose Café" is for Aleda Shirley, with thanks.

For their friendship and encouragement, my thanks to Jeff Carpenter, John Hoppenthaler, Dean Young, David Wojahn and Peter Cameron, as well as my colleagues and students at West Virginia University.

My gratitude to Walt and Phoebe for their endless inspiration.

Thanks also to the National Endowment for the Arts for a fellowship that aided in the completion of this book, and to the Eberly College of Arts and Sciences at West Virginia University for its longstanding support.

As always, this book would not exist in its present form without the invaluable assistance of Linda Warren, designer of beautiful books. And, of course, it wouldn't exist at all were it not for Jerry Costanzo, publisher extraordinaire.

Finally and most of all: Thank you, Amanda.

ABOUT THE AUTHOR

PHOTO BY AMANDA COBB

James Harms is the author of four earlier books from Carnegie Mellon University Press, Freeways and Aqueducts, Quarters, The Joy Addict *and* Modern Ocean. *His awards include a National Endowment for the Arts Fellowship, three Pushcart Prizes, and the PEN/Revson Fellowship. He lives with his wife, Amanda Cobb, and their children in Morgantown, West Virginia, where he teaches at West Virginia University.*

ABOUT THE BOOK

The text of After West *is set in Hightower (1994), designed by Tobias Frere-Jones, and Freehand 521 (1934), designed by Robert H. Middleton for Ludlow. This book was designed by Linda Warren at Studio Deluxe, Culver City, California. It was printed and bound by Jeff Carpenter of Westcott Press, Altadena, California.*